Read & Respond

FOR KS1

D1439656

Read & Respond

FOR KS1

Author: Janet Perry

Development Editor: Simret Brar

Editor: Roanne Charles

Assistant Editor: Vicky Butt

Series Designer: Anna Oliwa

Designer: Q2A Media

Illustrations: Patrick Benson

Text © 2008 Janet Perry © 2008 Scholastic Ltd

Designed using Adobe InDesign
Published by Scholastic Ltd, Villiers House,
Clarendon Avenue, Leamington Spa,
Warwickshire CV32 5PR
www.scholastic.co.uk

Printed by Bell & Bain
1 2 3 4 5 6 7 8 9   8 9 0 1 2 3 4 5 6 7

British Library Cataloguing-in-Publication Data
A catalogue record for this book is available from the British
Library.
ISBN 978-1407-10000-5

Acknowledgements

The publishers gratefully acknowledge permission to reproduce
the following copyright material: **Patrick Benson** for the use of
illustrations from *Read and Respond: Owl Babies* by Sue Palmer,
illustrations © 2000, Patrick Benson (2000, Scholastic Limited).
Walker Books Limited for the use of extracts from *Owl Babies*
by Martin Waddell and illustration by Patrick Benson © 1992,
Martin Waddell (1992, Walker Books Ltd., London SE11 5HJ).
Every effort has been made to trace copyright holders for the
works reproduced in this book, and the publishers apologise for
any inadvertent omissions.

Owl Babies

About the book

Owl Babies introduces three baby owls who wake up one night to find that their mother is not with them. The three worried little owls sit and think and talk to each other about where she has gone, and finally make a wish for their mother to return. Their wish comes true and their mother soon returns to their tree-trunk home.

The story is written in an accessible and engaging style using simple sentences and refrains, and fits into the genre of stories with patterned language. As the three owls sit and think and wait, their characters begin to emerge. Young readers readily join in with their comments, particularly those of the youngest owl, Bill, who always speaks last. The owls' simple statements help to build up a sense of suspense as they wait in the dark wood. Children will identify with the nervousness of waiting and feel their relief when their owl mother returns.

The text is ideal for reading aloud for both group and independent reading. The deceptive simplicity of the story is excellent for building confidence, and there are many opportunities to develop reading with expression. The characters of the owls themselves, the setting and the development of the plot are all instrumental in developing this skill. The uncomplicated structure of the story with its simple repetition links *Owl Babies* with PNS English objectives for Years 1 and 2.

Essential to a full appreciation of the book are Patrick Benson's beautiful and sensitive illustrations which give immediate insight into the world of the baby owls. The atmosphere of the wood at night and the expressive faces of the small owls add an extra dimension to the story. Many of the illustrations can be used for encouraging observation or for group discussion.

About the author

Martin Waddell lives in the area in which he was born near the mountains of Mourne in Northern Ireland. His love of stories began as a small boy from his experiences of having tales read to him by people who knew how to read them well. This sense of a story being alive is very much part of his own writing.

Many of his stories are based on personal experiences he has had near his home by the sea. He describes himself as 'a happy man'. He has survived being blown up and being buried alive and has overcome cancer. Such events have left their mark, but there is a sense of optimism and warmth shining through most of his stories.

Waddell 'dreams' his stories in his garden and on long walks on the beach by his house. He tells his stories to his dog before settling down to write them in the stone barn beside his house.

A familiar and popular writer, he is widely regarded as one of the finest contemporary storytellers for children and young people. His stories are always powerful, ranging from *Owl Babies*, *Farmer Duck*, the Little Bear series and *Once There Were Giants* to his trilogy for young people based on living in a troubled Northern Ireland.

Facts and figures
Owl Babies
Author: Martin Waddell
Illustrator: Patrick Benson
First published 1992 by Walker Books Ltd.
Martin Waddell has over 90 titles to his name.
Patrick Benson has illustrated over 24 titles.

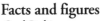

Guided reading

The cover

Look together at the front cover of the book.

Ask the children to point to the title of the book and then read it to you. Then ask the children to point to the two names underneath the title. Why do they think two names are there? Talk about the roles of author and illustrator.

Encourage the children to talk about the picture on the cover. Remind them that they have read the title, and ask them who they think the birds might be.

Ask the children to share what they know about owls. Then ask them to say what they have noticed about the owls in the picture, encouraging them to use descriptive language. How do we know what time of day it is?

Look at the back cover, and tell the children that the writing on the back of a book is called the 'blurb'. Ask them to repeat the word together. Explain that the blurb usually tells potential readers about the story and also what other readers thought about the book when they read it. Ask the children to point to the larger print and read it with them. Ask the children what they have discovered about the owls. Is it what they expected from looking at the front cover? Finally, ask the children to suggest what the smaller writing might be about.

First reading

Throughout the first full reading encourage the children to enjoy the developing story and join in if they wish to. On subsequent occasions focus on particular areas of the story as discussed in the sections below.

Three baby owls

Begin to set the context for the story by looking at the double page inside the cover. Ask the children why they think the spread has a pattern on it. Explain that it is part of one of the illustrations in the story. Help the children to talk about what the illustrator, Patrick Benson, might want us to think about when we look at this double page.

Turn to the title page and read the title together. Ask the children to comment on the picture here. Encourage them to describe what they can see and to predict what might happen.

Now begin reading, encouraging the children to join in. Pause to ask the children to speculate on the names of the owls. Which owl do they think is Sarah? Which might be Percy, and Bill? Can they think of any good words to describe the baby owls? How would they describe the mother owl? What would they say she is doing in the picture?

Invite the children to tell you all that they know about the owl family so far before you turn to the next page and read it together. Draw the children's attention to the word 'GONE'. Why do they think it is in capital letters? Model reading the owls' responses to this situation. Ask the children to look at the punctuation and encourage them to explain the difference between using a question mark and an exclamation mark. Ask the children to read the page again, looking carefully at the punctuation to help them with appropriate expression.

Examine the illustration together. What do the children think the two bigger owls are doing? Why do they think they are standing like that? What might baby Bill be thinking? If they look at the picture closely, are they reminded what owls use to make their homes?

Waiting

Continue to read the following page. Focus on the word 'thought'. Does it look different from the other words? Explain that it is printed in a different way so that we say it differently, with special emphasis. Can the children remember another place in the story where we have done this before?

Practise reading the first phrase together. Then ask the children to look at the next line. How does it look different from the others? Explain that these marks are called brackets and that they are used when a writer wants to tell the reader an extra piece of information. Practise reading the first two lines together. Then ask the children where they think the mother owl has gone. Do they agree with what Sarah and Bill say?

Ask the children to point to what Bill and Percy say. Can they remember what the marks are called at the end of the sentence? Try reading the owls' sentences with different children taking a part each. Move on to explore the illustration and challenge the children to think of words to describe what the owls are doing.

Turn to the next page and ask the children if they notice anything different about the content of this picture. (The owls are outside the tree.) Read the page together then return to the picture and ask the children to look at each owl in turn. What are they doing? Does the middle owl look as if he or she is going to say something? Ask the children to suggest which owl this might be and what he or she might be saying to Bill.

Read the first sentence on the next page and ask the children to point out each owl as they read. Can they say why Sarah is shown on the biggest branch and why Bill is on the ivy? Pause to ask the children if they know any more stories about three animals (such as 'Goldilocks and the Three Bears', 'The Three Little Pigs' and so on).

Read the conversation together, reminding the children of the emphasis on 'soon'. How is Sarah behaving towards her two smaller brothers? Can the children explain why Bill says 'I want my mummy' every time.

Look at the next page. What is noticeable about the owls in the picture? (They look very small.) Encourage the children to think of words to describe the wood at night. Then read the first sentence. Ask the children to read it again, taking particular notice of the word 'moved'. Encourage the children to suggest what might be moving in the wood at night. Read the rest of the page and practise putting expression into the owls' conversation.

Thinking

Turn to the following page and ask the children to look carefully at the illustration. How is it different from the last picture? (We can see the owls more clearly now and they are all sitting on the same branch.) Let the children think for a little while (like the owls!). Can they suggest what might have happened to make the owls want to sit together? Before reading the whole page, ask the children if they can see any words which they should say in a special way. Which owl says these words? Read the page together and ask the children why Bill and Percy do what Sarah says.

Wishing

Read the next page. Can the children suggest how the owls are feeling? What else might have happened to the mother owl? Share ideas. Ask the children to look at the picture and say how they know the owls are wishing really hard. What clues are there in the picture? Now encourage the children to predict what might happen next.

Turn to the following page and ask the children if they can think of any reasons why the three words here are so important. Challenge them to think of words to describe how the mother owl is flying through the wood. Then turn to the next page and read it together. Ask the children what they notice about the description of the mother owl flying through the trees. Invite the children to suggest other phrases which could be used to give a similar effect. What might the owl be thinking when she notices her babies sitting out on the branch?

At last

Read the next page together, then practise reading it again with expression. Ask the children to explain how they can tell that the baby owls are happy now. Which little owl do they think is the most excited? Why do they think this? Can they suggest any other words that could describe what the babies are doing? Can they think of words to describe the expression on the mother owl's face?

Read on to the following page. Invite different children to read the first line spoken by the mother owl. How would they read her next line, which is not written in capital letters? How do they think she might be feeling? Encourage the children to describe how the baby owls might be feeling (happy, relieved and so on). Ask the children if they can remember why brackets are used; but what is different about Bill's sentence this time? Encourage them to think about Percy's sentence. In the

rest of the story, what does he always say after Sarah has spoken?

Finally, encourage the children to think back over the whole story. Do they think the mother owl had been away for a long time? Did it just seem a long time because the baby owls were surprised that she had gone and because they were on their own?

Shared reading

Extract 1

- Read the extract on photocopiable page 8.
- Re-read and discuss the opening line with the children. Does 'Once there were' remind them of similar first words in any other stories? Read the line once more and note the number of owls. Do the children know any other stories about three animals ('The Three Little Pigs', for example)? Depending on the stories they suggest, explain that these are traditional tales or fairy stories that have been told for hundreds of years. *Owl Babies* is quite a new story. Can the children remember the name of the author? Do they know any of his other stories?
- Read the whole page again and ask the children to say what this opening description tells us about owls in general. Invite the children to share other facts they know about owls.
- Ask the children to trace each sentence on the page. Can they suggest why the last sentence is the shortest one?
- Look at the accompanying illustration and ask the children if they can tell which of the owls might be Sarah, Percy and Bill. What do they think the baby owls are thinking about?

Extract 2

- Read the second extract, on photocopiable page 9, to the children.
- Then tell the children that they are going to use this part of the story, which makes use of dialogue, to practise reading with expression. Model expressive reading of the first sentence, pausing after the comma and emphasising 'moved' which is presented in italic to show that it should be stressed. Talk about this with the children and read the page together.
- Discuss how the owls could be brave. Ask the children to imagine that, they are the owls. What will they do to look after each other?
- Ask the children to suggest what they think might be moving in the wood: perhaps leaves rustling, woodland creatures scurrying about. Make a list of these together.
- Re-read together the conversation between the owls. Ask the children how they could read it with more expression. Encourage different volunteers to demonstrate by reading the individual owls' words.
- Now ask the children to find a sentence that contains words that rhyme (Sarah's speech). Can they think of other words that fit this rhyme? ('Dice' and 'twice', for example.)

Extract 3

- Display the third extract, on photocopiable page 10. Point to the words of the text while reading it through with the children.
- Ask the children why the mother owl's first words are in capital letters. How do they think the mother owl is feeling as she arrives back to see her frightened babies? Re-read the lines of dialogue with appropriate expression and tone.
- Read the middle section. Invite the children to suggest why brackets are being used. (As an aside.) Encourage the children to share ideas as to what the owls might be thinking about.
- Now ask the children to look closely at what the owls are saying. Ask them to identify the speech marks and the exclamation marks. Can they explain why Sarah's sentences are different from the other owls' sentences?
- Read the whole extract again, paying attention to using expression, particularly in the conversation.

Extract 1

Once there were three baby owls:
Sarah and Percy and Bill.
They lived in a hole
in the trunk of a tree
with their Owl Mother.
The hole had twigs and
leaves and owl feathers in it.
It was their house.

Text © 1992, Martin Waddell. Illustration © 2000, Patrick Benson.

Extract 2

It was dark in the wood and
They had to be brave, for things
moved all around them.
"She'll bring us mice and
things that are nice," said Sarah.
"I suppose so!" said Percy.
"I want my mummy!" said Bill.

Text © 1992, Martin Waddell; Illustration © 2000, Patrick Benson.

Extract 3

"WHAT'S ALL THE FUSS?"
their Owl Mother asked.
"You knew I'd come back."
The baby owls thought
(all owls think a lot) –
"I knew it," said Sarah.
"And I knew it!" said Percy.
"I love my mummy!" said Bill.

Text © 1992, Martin Waddell; Illustration © 2000 , Patrick Benson.

SCHOLASTIC
www.scholastic.co.uk

Plot, character and setting

True or false?

> **Objective:** To recall information gathered from the text and illustrations.
> **What you need:** Photocopiable page 15, scissors, glue.
> **Cross-curricular links:** PHSE.

What to do
● Tell the children they are going to play a game with a partner. Each player will take a turn to make three statements about the story. If their partner believes the sentence is true, they will give a 'thumbs up' sign. If the sentence is false (not true), they will give a 'thumbs down' sign.
● Explain that the class will play the game together first so that everyone understands what to do. Make a true statement about the story, such as 'Bill is the smallest owl', and ask the children to signal whether they think it is true or false. Repeat with a false statement, such as 'The story is called *Rabbit Babies*'. Tell the children that the false statements they give must be about the characters or something connected with the story.
● Let the children play the game, and then spend a short time taking feedback.
● Show the children the photocopiable page, telling them it works in the same way as the game: they should read the statements and decide if they are true or false, then cut them out and stick them in the correct column.

> **Differentiation**
> **For older/more confident learners:** Encourage children to add their own statements. They can then invent their own card game and write out the rules.
> **For younger/less confident learners:** Let children make their decisions with a partner.

Remembering

> **Objective:** To understand time and sequential relationships in a story.
> **What you need:** Photocopiable page 16, writing and drawing materials, flipchart and pen.
> **Cross-curricular links:** Art and design.

What to do
● Ask the children if they know what the word 'sequence' means? Explain that if they can put the events from a story in the right order (or sequence), it shows that they understand and remember the story correctly.
● Challenge the children to recall the beginning of the story. What is the first thing they remember? (We meet the owl family.)
● Write 'First' on the flipchart, followed by one of the children's answers as to the first thing from the story.
● Explain to the children that we need some more headings on the flipchart to help us put the story in order. Invite the children to suggest further time headings, such as 'Next', 'Then' and 'After that', and write these on the flipchart. Ask the children what the final heading will be. ('Finally', 'At last' or 'In the end'.)
● Work through these headings, with the children suggesting a sentence to write under each one. Explain that the same information can be given in different ways and discuss alternative versions as the children suggest them.
● Explain how to complete the photocopiable page, asking the children to use their own words and to complete each box with a careful illustration.

> **Differentiation**
> **For older/more confident learners:** Remove the sentence starters before photocopying the sheet and ask for more complex sentences.
> **For younger/less confident learners:** Provide adult support for group work, discussing each section before writing.

Plot, character and setting

Meet the owls

Objective: To describe characters using text and illustrations and expressing their own views.
What you need: Copies of *Owl Babies*, photocopiable page 17, writing materials, soft pencils, individual whiteboards and pens.
Cross-curricular links: Science: living things.

What to do

● Read the opening page of the book together and invite the children to say what they know about the owls.
● Encourage the children to look closely at the illustration and offer more information about the owls, for example that they don't look like their mother; there is a little owl; and so on.
● Ask the children to write on their whiteboards a list of words that describe the owls, such as 'soft feathers', 'pointed beaks'. Share some examples.
● Encourage the children to close their eyes

and choose an owl from the story. Tell them to think of everything they know about that character.
● Ask the children to write their ideas on their whiteboards and share examples. Encourage others to work out who has been written about.
● Show the children the photocopiable page and explain that they are going to use the words on their whiteboards to write about each owl.
● They should describe each owl and give one example from the story that supports their description.

Differentiation
For older/more confident learners: Ask the children to research different types of owl as an extension activity.
For younger/less confident learners: Provide adult support for small groups to discuss word choices. Ask children to write about one or two characters only.

Story ingredients

Objectives: To identify parts of a story; to reflect on the structure of a the story.
What you need: Copies of *Owl Babies*, photocopiable page 18, writing materials, flipchart and pen, sets of word cards with 'Beginning', 'Middle' and 'Ending'.

What to do

● Ask the children if they know what an author needs to do before he or she writes a story. Encourage the children to share what they know about the writing process, for example writing the beginning, the middle, the ending, a crisis and resolution, characters. List their ideas as key words on the flipchart.
● Remind the children of the times they have planned a story and ask them to explain how they do this. Are there any parts of story planning

which they find easier to do than others? Which parts do they find difficult? Why? Refer to the list on the flipchart.
● Tell the children that you are going to read the story again and that they are going to hold up a card to indicate each different section of the story. Give out the word cards.
● Read the story and ask the children to hold up the correct card as the story progresses.
● Now show the children the photocopiable page and discuss the headings in each section. Ask for some examples and make sure the children understand what to do.

Differentiation
For older/more confident learners: Encourage children to work on a more complex story.
For younger/less confident learners: Let children work in pairs.

Plot, character and setting

A letter to a friend

> **Objective:** To express views about a story.
> **What you need:** Individual whiteboards and pens, paper and writing materials, flipchart and pen.
> **Cross-curricular links:** ICT: word processing.

What to do
● Tell the children that they are going to write a letter about *Owl Babies* to a friend in another class.
● Ask the children to use their whiteboards to note down some words to describe the book. Invite the children to share these with the rest of the class and list them on the flipchart.
● Ask the children what other information should go in the letter. Does the person they are sending the letter to need to know *everything* about the story? What could they include to make their friend want to read it? List useful phrases on the flipchart.

● Ask the children to note on their whiteboards their favourite part of the story, then what they think is the most important part of the story. Share these ideas.
● Remind the children that they need to include some details about the plot, characters and setting.
● Write 'I would recommend this book because…' as a sentence starter on the flipchart, choosing children to complete the sentence orally.
● Remind the children of the conventions of letter writing before giving out the paper or using the computer.

> **Differentiation**
> **For older/more confident learners:** Look for the use of more complex sentences and vocabulary.
> **For younger/less confident learners:** Provide a writing frame or computer template in letter format.

What the owls say

> **Objective:** To investigate story dialogue.
> **What you need:** Copies of *Owl Babies*, at least four paper speech bubbles per group, writing materials.

What to do
● Hold up a paper speech bubble and ask the children if they know what it is called. Have they seen them used in cartoons or in other stories?
● Explain to the children that they are going to work in groups of four in which each person will be a character from the book.
● Ask the children to organise themselves into groups of four and decide quickly who will be mother owl, Sarah, Percy and Bill.
● Tell the children that they are going to have a conversation as the characters from the story. Explain that they can choose a conversation from the book, or they can think of something that

the owl family *might* talk about together. Each group member will say a sentence which will be written on a speech bubble later.
● Check that each group has the correct characters. Give the children a short time to decide what their family conversation will be about before rehearsing their sentences.
● Give out the speech bubbles and ask each child to write down their line of dialogue. Ask each group to read their dialogue to each other.
● Give out more speech bubbles so that the conversation can be extended.
● Invite the groups to share their work.

> **Differentiation**
> **For older/more confident learners:** Expect complex sentences and a longer dialogue. Encourage reading with expression.
> **For younger/less confident learners:** Suggest children use a conversation from the book, supported by an adult.

Plot, character and setting

What happens in the story?

> **Objective:** To summarise the plot of a story.
> **What you need:** Copies of *Owl Babies*, A4 paper folded into three, small sticky notes (three per child), writing materials, a set of large word cards with 'Beginning', 'Middle' and 'Ending', Blue Tack®, flipchart and pen.

What to do
- Draw two horizontal lines on the flipchart to make three sections. Tell the children that later, when they start their writing, they will be using three sections like these.
- Ask the children if they know what the word 'plot' means. Elicit or explain that the plot is what happens in a story.
- Read the story to the children.
- Hold up the word cards to the children and attach the 'Beginning' card to the top section of the flipchart. Ask the children to suggest sentences that could be written in this section. Write them up, checking with the children.
- Continue in the same way with the middle section, asking the children for ideas and checking that the sequence is correct. Put the 'Ending' word card in place, but don't complete this section.
- Give the children their three sticky notes and ask them to write 'Beginning', 'Middle' and 'Ending' as on the flipchart. Ask the children to fix their sticky-note headings in the correct sections on their paper.
- Now ask them to write sentences in all three sections to summarise the story.

> **Differentiation**
> **For older/more confident learners:** Invite children to summarise a more detailed book without mentioning the title and ask a partner to guess the book.
> **For younger/less confident learners:** Provide sentence starters for each section.

The wood at night

> **Objective:** To describe the setting of a story.
> **What you need:** Copies of *Owl Babies*, the outline of a tree drawn on the flipchart, A3 paper with the same outline (one per pair), pieces of paper shaped like leaves, glue, writing and drawing materials.
> **Cross-curricular links:** Science: light and dark.

What to do
- Ask the children if they can remember what we mean when we talk about the 'setting' in a story. Where is *Owl Babies* set?
- Turn to the picture showing the tiny owls in the big dark wood. Prompt the children to think of words they could use to describe the wood. Share these words and write them in the tree shape on the flipchart.
- Read the first sentence on this page, and ask *Why is the word 'moved' in different print? What do you think you might hear moving in the wood?* Add these words to the others.
- Challenge the children to think of other movement words which could be put in the tree shape, such as 'scampering', and add these.
- Ask the children to find a partner. Then give each pair some leaf shapes and the A3 tree outline. Tell the children to write descriptive words on the leaves and phrases around the tree. Then let them stick the leaves down to complete their picture of the owls' tree at night.

> **Differentiation**
> **For older/more confident learners:** Encourage children to use more descriptive phrases.
> **For younger/less confident learners:** Play a cumulative circle game: 'In the dark wood I can see…'

True or false?

Are these statements true or false?

True	False

Sarah looked after Bill and Percy.	The mother owl stayed with the baby owls.
The owls went to look for their mother.	The owls lived in a nest.
Owls think a lot.	Percy perched on the ivy.
The owls danced when their mother came home.	The owls had to be brave.

Plot, character and setting

SECTION
4

Remembering

Use the words at the bottom of the page to write and then draw what happens in the story, in the correct order.

First Three baby owls lived in a tree with their mother.	

Next	At last	After that	Finally	Then

Plot, character and setting

Meet the owls

What do you know about the owls in the story?
Name and describe each owl.

Mother Owl	Sarah
Discription _____	Discription _____
_____	_____
_____	_____
_____	_____
_____	_____
Examples _____	Examples _____
_____	_____

Percy	Bill
Discription _____	Discription _____
_____	_____
_____	_____
_____	_____
_____	_____
Examples _____	Examples _____
_____	_____

Illustration © 2000, Patrick Benson.

SECTION
4

Story ingredients

How is the story put together?

Title	
Characters	**Setting** (where the story happens)
Events (what happens in the story)	**Ending**

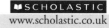
www.scholastic.co.uk

Talk about it

Tell it again

> **Objective:** To retell a story, ordering events and using story language.
> **What you need:** Photocopiable page 22, writing and colouring materials, art straws or dowels, sticky tape, flipchart and pen, laminator.
> **Cross-curricular links:** Drama; design and technology.

What to do
● Tell the children that they are going to retell the story with puppets which they will make.
● Ask the children to help you list the events in the story, writing each one on the flipchart. When all the events have been listed, ask the children to check that they are in the right order, then read them through together.
● Arrange the children into groups of four and ask them to decide which characters from the story they will be.
● Show the children the photocopiable page.

Tell them that it is important to use appropriate storytelling words during their performance. Ask them which words they will use to start their story. Can they think of any others to put in the box?
● When the box is complete, ask each group to rehearse their story, making sure they use the words.
● Finally, ask the children to colour the owl shapes carefully, front and back.
● Let the children rehearse again, this time with their puppets, and have the owls laminated before the final performance.

> **Differentiation**
> **For older/more confident learners:** Challenge children to use the puppets to create a sequel.
> **For younger/less confident learners:** Provide word cards with story language and let children use these to retell part of the story.

Caring

> **Objective:** To develop themes from a story.
> **What you need:** Space for circle time, circle time object, photocopiable page 23, writing materials.
> **Cross-curricular links:** PSHE: caring for others, showing empathy.

What to do
● Organise circle time, explaining to the children that this session is about the *Owl Babies* story. Say, 'We are going to think about caring for others'.
● Hold up the circle time object and tell the children that you will pass it around and only the person holding it may speak. Start by making a statement for example, 'Sarah looked after Percy and Bill'. Continue around the circle, passing on the object and encouraging the children to say something about the three baby owls.
● Encourage the children to think about a similar time when someone has been kind to them. Model this with an example: 'Alex looked

after Asif when he fell over…'. Continue around the circle, encouraging the children to speak from personal experience.
● Now ask the children to think about people who are caring and how they behave. Invite them to complete the sentence 'A caring person…' ('always listens', 'is kind' and so on). Continue around the circle.
● Can the children think about how *they* could be more caring? Model the statement 'I can be caring…'.
● Finally, explain the photocopiable page, conclude circle time in the usual way and let the children work on the sheet.

> **Differentiation**
> **For older/more confident learners:** Set children the task of designing a poster about caring.
> **For younger/less confident learners:** Let children sit close to you during circle time then work in pairs.

Talk about it

Owls think a lot

> **Objective:** To identify and discuss characters' feelings.
> **What you need:** Copies of *Owl Babies*, photocopiable page 24, writing materials, flipchart and pen.
> **Cross-curricular links:** PSHE.

What to do
● Ask the children to say what the young owls do during the story (they wait, they think, they wish).
● Tell the children that you are going to talk together about how the baby owls might be feeling. In the middle of the story, are they worried? Why did they go and sit on the branch outside their home in the tree?
● We know from the story that owls think a lot. Do the children think that the owls all have the same thoughts?
● Ask the children to turn to a partner and say what they know about Sarah. Can they say what Sarah might be thinking at particular points in the story?
● Invite the children to share their ideas and then repeat the activity for Percy and Bill.
● Look at the front cover of the book and ask the children how we could show what the owls are thinking about. (They may suggest speech bubbles.) Draw a large speech bubble on the flipchart, then draw a thought bubble. Encourage the children to explain the difference and when each should be used.
● Look at the illustration of mother owl flying back and ask the children to suggest her thought(s). Write one in the thought bubble on the flipchart.
● Hand out the photocopiable page, asking the children to write thoughts for each owl.

> **Differentiation**
> **For older/more confident learners:** Ask children to make more bubbles for extra thoughts.
> **For younger/less confident learners:** Provide adult support for rehearsal before writing.

Ask me

> **Objective:** To identify characters in role and explore characterisation.
> **What you need:** Teacher copy of *Owl Babies*, chair for hot-seating.
> **Cross-curricular links:** Drama.

What to do
● Sit on the chair in front of the children. Say you are a character in a story and the children can take turns to ask you questions about yourself (hot-seating). Choose a character from a fairy tale or a story which is a class favourite. Tell the children who you are and give them time to think of questions, then invite their questions, remembering to answer in role.
● Now tell the children that you are going to read *Owl Babies* to them. Before you start, tell them that they need to listen really well and think about some questions they could ask a character from the story. Suggest that their questions can be about the characters' feelings, their behaviour or about something that happened in the story.
● After reading, ask for a volunteer to sit in the hot seat in role as a character from the story. Explain that each person in the hot seat can only answer four questions. Ask the 'character' to choose children who are ready with questions. Remind the character that all the answers must be in role.
● Choose other volunteers to sit in the hot seat.

> **Differentiation**
> **For older/more confident learners:** Challenge children to take on the imaginary role of another animal in the wood.
> **For younger/less confident learners:** Devise questions with a partner.

Talk about it

5

How would they say it?

Objective: To act out a story using different voices for characters.
What you need: Large space, mini whiteboard and pen for each group.
Cross-curricular links: Drama.

What to do
● Organise the children into groups of four, each sitting in a semicircle. Tell the children they are going to be characters in *Owl Babies*. Ask each group to list the characters on their whiteboard and select one to be.
● Tell the groups to discuss each character in turn, ensuring all of the children have a chance to say what they know about each one.
● Ask the children to consider how their character would speak. For example, would Bill have a loud, confident voice?
● Let the children talk in their groups to practise using their owl voices. Circulate to listen and comment where necessary.

● Ask for volunteers to demonstrate their characters' ways of speaking.
● Now ask the children how they can become even more like the birds, and focus on the idea of movement. Invite suggestions about how the owls in the story move. Do they all fly? What other movements do they (and other birds) make? Give the groups time to rehearse these.
● Give each group time to think about how they will act out the story and suggest they use their whiteboard to note down ideas. Remind them to be aware of the story's setting and how this might affect their ideas.
● Allow ample rehearsal time, supporting where necessary, before asking the groups to share their work.

Differentiation
For older/more confident learners: Challenge groups to devise a prequel to the story.
For younger/less confident learners: Ask groups to act out a conversation between two of the characters.

The owls' world

Objective: To discuss a story setting in a small group.
What you need: A2 paper for each group, writing materials.
Cross-curricular links: Science, art and design.

What to do
● Tell the children that they are going to turn part of the classroom into the place where the owl babies lived. Invite them to share what they know about the setting of the story.
● Explain to the children that they are going to be working in small groups to discuss and make plans together.
● Organise the children into small groups and give out the paper. Choose a scribe for each group to write down the groups' ideas.
● Ask the groups to discuss how they can

decorate the area and recreate the story setting – the wood. What materials would they need? Ask the children to consider if any signs or labels would be needed. What would be written on these?
● Then ask the children to discuss the characters. Will they make them, use toys or puppets, or be the characters themselves? Circulate and prompt where necessary.
● Finally, invite each group to share their ideas. Discuss with the children how you could incorporate some ideas from each group.

Differentiation
For older/more confident learners: Let children work independently to plan a wood inside a shoebox. Encourage them to share the process with the class.
For younger/less confident learners: Create a table-top small-world version of the wood.

PAGE
21

READ & RESPOND: Activities based on Owl Babies

Tell it again

Words to use when we tell the story:

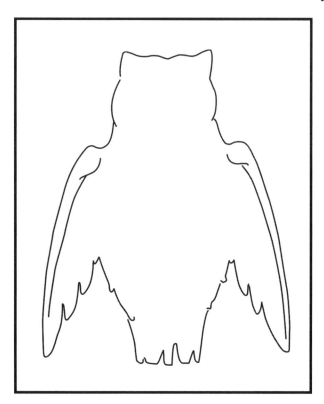

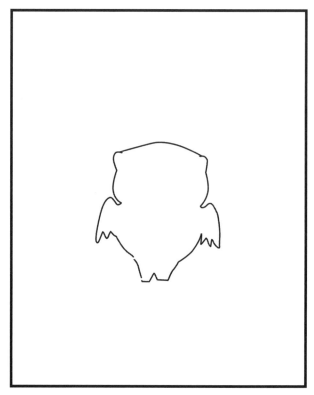

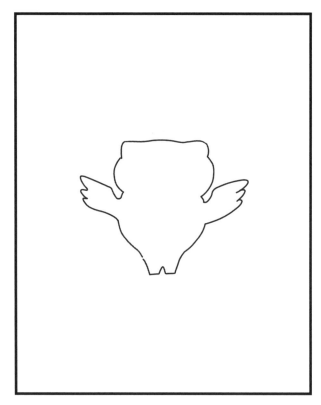

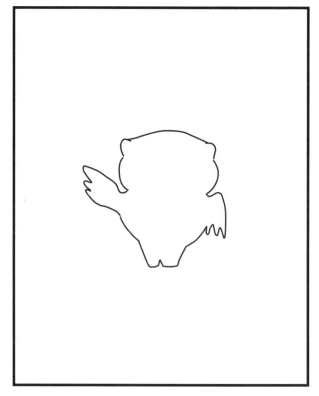

SECTION
5

Caring

Think about kindness and fill out the sections below.

_____ was kind to me when _____

I was helpful when _____

Four ways to be caring and helpful at home

1 _____

2 _____

3 _____

4 _____

Four ways to be caring and helpful at school

1 _____

2 _____

3 _____

4 _____

Draw a picture to show you can be caring.

Talk about it

Owls think a lot

What are they thinking?

Illustration © 2000 Patrick Benson.

Get writing

Owl facts

> **Objective:** To read and write non-fiction text.
> **What you need:** Photocopiable page 28, a range of non-fiction sources – print and electronic – featuring birds and woodland creatures, paper, writing and drawing materials, flipchart and pen.
> **Cross-curricular links:** Science: Living things in the environment; Humans and other animals.

What to do

● Show the children the books and ask them if they can tell you how they are different from the *Owl Babies* book. Can they tell a big difference just by looking at the cover? Ask: *What do we call books that are not story books? How do we use non-fiction books?*

● Tell the children that they are going to write a report about owls. First, they are going to think about the facts that they already know about owls and where they live. Then they are going to collect more information

● Invite the children to suggest facts about owls to write on the flipchart, for example that they fly at night. Discuss these with the whole class.

● Ask the children if they know the best way to collect information (from several sources).

● Read the headings on the photocopiable sheet and explain how to complete each section. Explain that this will help to plan their report.

● Let the children do their research, using the school library, a topic pack, CD-ROM or selected websites.

● Ask the children to check their notes carefully. Ask them to write their reports and include illustrations if possible.

> **Differentiation**
> **For older/more confident learners:** Help children to produce a detailed leaflet about woodland animals.
> **For younger/less confident learners:** Provide adult support for sharing research in small groups.

And after that…

> **Objective:** To use a story's characters and setting in new story writing.
> **What you need:** Copies of *Owl Babies*, photocopiable page 29, writing materials, individual whiteboards and pens, flipchart and pen.

What to do

● Turn to the final picture in the book. Read the accompanying text with the children and then ask them to think about what might happen next. Ask the children to turn to a partner and say what the owls might do or say next. Then invite the children to share their ideas.

● Tell the children that they are going to write a new story about the owls and their mother set after Martin Waddell's story ends. Ask the children if the story would happen in the day or at night. Why would night time be best?

● Ask the children to turn to their partner again and discuss ideas for an owl babies story.

● Write the words 'Beginning', 'Middle' and 'Ending' spaced out on the flipchart. Ask the children to say how they would use these headings to plan their own stories. Write some of the ideas on the flipchart in the appropriate section.

● Now show and explain the the photocopiable page. Encourage the children to talk about the way their story might begin, and ask them to suggest interesting opening sentences.

> **Differentiation**
> **For older/more confident learners:** Encourage children to include more dialogue and introduce a new character.
> **For younger/less confident learners:** Arrange for children to work in a small group with an adult to support writing.

Get writing

Night writing

Objective: To develop descriptive writing.
What you need: Copies of *Owl Babies*, photocopiable page 30, writing materials, flipchart and pen.

What to do
● Tell the children that they are going to create a piece of writing which describes a particular place. Explain that it is important that they use the most interesting and precise words that they can think of when they begin their writing.
● Turn to the double-page spread in *Owl Babies* showing the wood at night. Give the children a little time to examine the illustration.
● Divide the flipchart into two and write 'Sights' in the first section. Ask the children to use the best words they can think of to describe what they can see in the picture. Encourage them to join words to make interesting and powerful phrases.
● Read through the words with the children and then invite them to add others describing what else they might see in a wood at night.
● Write 'Sounds' in the next section on the flipchart. Ask the children to close their eyes and imagine the sounds they might hear in a wood at night. Invite them to share these and write them down as before. Read the words together.
● Explain the photocopiable page and read the sentence starters with them. Remind the children to combine interesting words to make effective descriptive phrases.
● If you have done the previous activity, 'And after that…', explain to the children how they could incorporate their setting description into the story.

Differentiation
For older/more confident learners: Ask children to write about a different place, for example a town, the sea and so on.
For younger/less confident learners: Provide further sentence starters based on the children's ideas.

Animal babies

Objective: To plan a story based on a familiar theme.
What you need: Paper and writing materials, individual whiteboards and pens, flipchart and pen.

What to do
● Tell the children that they are going to write a story about an animal family. They can choose to write about any type of animal that they know something about.
● Ask the children to choose their animal and write the appropriate title such as 'Rabbit Babies' on their whiteboards, then write the names of their characters underneath.
● Tell the children to write about the setting. Where does the story happen? Does it take place in the daytime or at night?
● Ask the children to suggest what else they need to think about when they plan their story. How will their story begin? Write 'Beginning' on the flipchart and note down suggestions the children make for story openings.
● Next, encourage the children to develop ideas for the main part of their story. Write these on the flipchart and discuss them.
● Repeat the process for the story ending.
● Ask the children to look at their whiteboards to develop their characters and setting and also to refer to the flipchart for story ideas.
● First, ask the children to write an interesting opening sentence on their whiteboard to share with the class, then let them complete their plans before starting to write out their stories.

Differentiation
For older/more confident learners: Help children to make and illustrate a small story book.
For younger/less confident learners: Suggest that children use familiar woodland characters.

Get writing

Make a wish

> **Objective:** To use an event from a story in new writing.
> **What you need:** Small pieces of coloured paper, writing and drawing materials.
> **Cross-curricular links:** PSHE: thinking about other people.

What to do

● Ask the children if they can remember what the owl babies did just before their mother came home. (They wished for her to come back.) Can they think of any other stories where wishes come true? (Cinderella wishing to go to the ball.)
● Are there any other times when they might make a wish, for instance when blowing out candles on a birthday cake? Discuss with the children how they make a wish.
● With care and sensitivity, encourage the children to talk about wishes they have made. Have any of them come true? Invite confident children to come to the front and share these happy experiences.
● Tell the children that they are going to make a class collection of wishes. The wishes could be for themselves, or for other people, perhaps even for people they have never met.
● Organise the children into a circle and invite them to think of someone they could make a wish for. Encourage them to think outside their own world to people who would really benefit from their wish. Model 'I wish for… because…' and continue around the circle.
● Ask the children to make three wishes, writing them down and decorating them. Display these as a class book or on a 'wish wall'.

> **Differentiation**
> **For older/more confident learners:** Prompt children to give extended reasons for their wishes.
> **For younger/less confident learners:** Ask children to write two wishes only.

Stories by Martin Waddell

> **Objective:** To compare stories written by the same author.
> **What you need:** Copies of *Owl Babies*, other books by Martin Waddell (one per group), A2 paper for each group with two columns – 'Similar' and 'Different', two large sticky notes for each child, writing materials, individual whiteboards and pens.

What to do

● Explain to the children that they are going to work in groups with a different book by Martin Waddell.
● Organise the children into small groups with at least one good reader in each group.
● Ask the children to work with a partner and write quick notes on their whiteboard about the characters in *Owl Babies*. Repeat this for the setting and events in the story.
● Give each group reader their other Martin Waddell book and tell the children to look at it carefully. When they hear the story, they should think of whether it is like *Owl Babies* or not.
● Give out two sticky notes to each child and ask them to write down one thing which is the same about the stories and one thing which is different.
● Ask the children to write the two book titles on their A2 paper and arrange the sticky notes underneath them in the appropriate columns.
● Take feedback from each group on how similar or different the stories are. Did the groups come up with a variety of points about the two stories?

> **Differentiation**
> **For older/more confident learners:** Write reviews comparing two Waddell books.
> **For younger/less confident learners:** Work in a small group with an adult reader.

Owl facts

Use these spaces to write down the information you have collected.

Different sorts of owls.	Where do owls live?

Other interesting owl facts.	What do owls eat?

Owls

Baby owls.	What do owls do?

■ SCHOLASTIC
www.scholastic.co.uk

And after that...

Use these spaces to plan a new owl babies story.

Characters	Setting

Beginning

Middle

Ending

SECTION
6

Night writing

Can you write interesting sentences to describe the night?

_____

_____

The night was as dark as

_____

_____

The stars were

_____

_____

The moon shone like

_____

_____

The branches were

_____

_____

The woodland animals were

_____

_____

The leaves were

_____

_____

Assessment

Assessment advice

Assessment will inform you of the level of progress being made by the children, and the outcomes arising from this assessment will then influence the development of future planning. It is essential that the children's learning is moved forward and that they receive the best and most appropriate level of support. The children themselves should be involved in their own assessment and target-setting and it is important that they feel very much a part of the development of their own learning.

By working through the lessons within this book, children are offered a variety of activities to develop their literacy skills, based around an accessible and engaging story. Reading and writing skills and speaking and listening skills can all be assessed by written and/or classroom observations. Some of the activities lend themselves to observation of group or paired work, while others require more personal creativity and imagination or writing techniques, for example, and are therefore more appropriate as an individual assessment. The assessment activity on photocopiable page 32 can be used to form part of a record of an individual child's progress and and thus inform your own or your colleagues' planning for future learning.

What do I know?

> **Objective:** To show understanding of a story.
> **What you need:** Photocopiable page 32, writing materials.

What to do
● For the most effective assessment, aim to combine verbal responses the children make during this session with written information gained afterwards using the photocopiable page.
● First, ask the children how we approach reading a new book. *What do we look at first? What information do we expect to find when we pick a book up? Where would we find this information?* (On the cover – front and back.)
● Invite the children to share their personal thoughts about the book. Which part of the story did they enjoy most? Do they have a favourite character? What would they say about the book to someone who had not read it?
● Encourage the children to say what an author needs to think about when writing a story. Invite them to talk about the characters, the plot and the setting. Also discuss how the illustrations contribute to the story.
● Invite the children to work with a partner and choose another story which is a class favourite. Encourage the children to discuss the plot, character and setting, and illustrations if appropriate, of this book. Move among the children to listen to their conversations.
● Return to focus on *Owl Babies* and talk in general about its features. Invite various children to talk about the characters, where the book is set, and events in the story. (Avoid going into great detail on any aspect as this may influence the children's written assessment.)
● Explain to the children that they are going to answer some questions connected with reading *Owl Babies* and with some of the work they have done about the story.
● Remind the children that they will be expected to use full sentences for their answers, with capital letters and full stops in the correct places.

What do I know?

What do you know about the book *Owl Babies*?
Remember to use full stops and capital letters in your sentences.

1. What are the names of the three baby owls?

_____

Illustration © 2000, Patrick Benson.

2. Where do the owls live?

_____

3. Which owl sat on the ivy branch?

_____

4. What did the owls wish for? Why?

_____

_____

5. Who said "I want my mummy!"

_____

6. What colour is the mother owl?

_____

7. Who wrote *Owl Babies*?

_____

8. Do you know another book by the same author?

_____